THE CRIMINAL, THE CROSS & THE CHURCH
THE INTERIOR JOURNEY

By

David H. Lukenbill

A Chulu Press Book

First Chulu Press Edition published
December 2008
ISBN-10 0-9791670-6-x
ISBN-13 978-0-9791670-6-5

Published by The Lampstand Foundation

www.lampstandfoundation.org

For Marlene & Erika Always

———— ··· ————

The penitential criminal working to reform other criminals, wisely spends the rest of his life atoning for the harm he has done during his criminal life; not because the world requires it, but because the eternal balance requires it, his immortal soul requires it, and God wishes it.

Contents

7

I- Preface

And further, that in terms of effective criminal reformation, it is only the transformed professional criminal who will be able to transform other criminals. The professional criminal who commits crimes for money—not the rapist, the pedophile, the thrill killer, and the other variants of offenders generally bundled up in one group when outsiders speak of criminals— offenders who are not safe within the maximum security prison where the ancient culture of the professional criminal that embodies the protection of the innocent, still endures and governs.

I-1) 𝕿his book is the final book of an initial three book series from the Lampstand Foundation—there will be other three book series—which began with *The Criminal's Search for God* and continued with *Carceral World, Communal City*; whose focus has been on the criminal world, the carceral influence, and now, in this final of the series, the interior journey of the penitential criminal working out his lifelong atonement within the Church, through the world, helping other criminals transform their lives.

I-2) My first two books were somewhat academic, replete with extended quotes from the *Catechism*, Early Church Fathers, the Holy Father, and Catholic scholars; providing an formal introduction to my essential premise: 'It takes a reformed criminal to reform criminals', and helping direct the penitential criminal to further study.

This final book of the series is simply my reflections on the criminal transformative work and the apostolate of the Lampstand Foundation within the social teaching principles of the Catholic Church.

I-3) It is virtually impossible to explain to the outside observer, regardless of their level of education or professional experience—even if that experience has been within the criminal justice system— the reality of living many years within the criminal world and the maximum security prison.

It is a reality that can only be approached by experiencing it (an experience—in terms of prison—no one chooses) and even for those working within the criminal justice system—with the freedom of being outside of either the criminal or carceral world— the guards, the prison workers, the administrators, and other law enforcement, legal, and correctional professionals, knowing the reality of it is just flat-out impossible, which is why my books are written for criminals, and will be best understood only by criminals.

I-4) And further, that in terms of effective criminal reformation, it is only the transformed professional criminal who will be able to transform other criminals. The professional criminal who commits crimes for money—not the rapist, the pedophile, the thrill killer, and the other variants of offenders generally bundled up in one group when outsiders speak of criminals— offenders who are not safe within the maximum security prison where the ancient culture of the professional criminal that embodies the protection of the innocent, still endures and governs.

Further still, it is only those professional criminals who have served time in maximum security prisons who are not informers, who can become powerful rehabilitative professionals; for they and they alone, can speak to all criminals in an authentic voice, calling them to transformation and reformation.

II- Introduction

The criminal carries the cross of his secret past, revealed in his capture, and brought to the light in his penitential life of atonement in the Church; the interior journey of a lifetime and the only apostolate worthy of such a life.

II-1) The experience of evil being turned to good through the grace of God is a wonderful tool vitally needed by the world; a world within which criminals grow and deepen their commitment to the evil of the criminal world as it becomes more congruent with the world it seeks to fully embrace, an embrace where, in some places, it has already done so.

What eventually attracts criminals into a lifetime commitment to the criminal world is clarity, excitement, truth, and honor—all of which are only trumped by living the sacramental life and deep study of the social teaching of the Catholic Church—the deepest well of clarity, excitement, truth, and honor in the history of the world.

Within the Catholic Church the criminal discovers the truth that the only response to his many years of being a criminal is to live the rest of his life following the path of sainthood, atoning for the harm he caused during his criminal life.

Criminals are so because of their distance from God and the beginning path to erasing that distance is only found in the Catholic Church—the only repository of truth in the world.

II-2) Just as the Catholic Church exploded in growth under the protection of the Roman Emperor Constantine, so today the Church continues its mission to become accepted and protected as the universal and only Church by all governments— finally removing from Satan's hands the principalities, thrones, powers, states, and combines through which so much of his evil is enacted.

II-3) Since the early part of the 20th Century the criminal world in the United States has grown into a sophisticated enterprise closely linked to the worlds of business and politics; and since the middle decades of that century, the carceral world has grown to exert a substantial level of control over the criminal world culture.

Consequently, any attempt to develop and manage programs that are able to perform the task of reforming criminals, must be able to have authentic access to them to have any hope of success.

Criminals are not reformed by programs alone, or by specific services doled out by bureaucratic structures; but by a change of heart, an internal decision that transforming their life has more and longer sustainable value than their current life as a criminal; a criminal life possessing tremendous value from both their lived and imagined perspective.

There was a period in America—from its founding until the 20th Century—when people of good will were able to successfully intervene in the lives of criminals and bring many of them to the transformative path, and there are reports of a 10% recidivist rate throughout that period.

However, once the pinnacle of the criminal and carceral world culture became an admirable and sought after height to scale—even within the public world—those relatively amateur attempts would no longer work and the results over the past decades reflect that.

The transformed professional criminal, who has come from the heights of the carceral criminal world, has retained his personal honor, has accomplished his professional goals of higher education, has received training in the intricacies of managing a nonprofit grassroots organization, and received in-depth training in the social teaching of the Catholic Church; and consequently, is one of the very few people who will be able to effectively reach and reform the criminal.

II-4) The master story behind the ability of the transformed criminal to help other criminals begin to transform their lives, is the voice of the least having value in the world of the great, the great whose authorship of the stories of rehabilitation are and have been for some time, completely and utterly false.

The experiences of the lowly matter more to the Catholic faith and the rehabilitative profession than those of the mighty, and it is from the voice of the lowly that the transformed criminal speaks, while the traditional rehabilitation practitioner speaks from the voice of the mighty; and the way of the mighty, the way of riches, position and standing, is suspect, as it largely results from a too successful congruence with the way of the world while disowning eternal truths.

III- Part One
The Criminal

The path is narrow, we must not forget. It is not a wide road full of comfort and ease, but a narrow one of struggle and the cross, though blessed with a joy beyond understanding only saints are fortunate to know and it is sainthood we must have for our goal.

Three Criminal Saints

Jesus Christ, the criminal, and the Catholic Church form a triptych held together by love, informed by charity, and realized by suffering.

III-1) There are three major criminal saints—St. Mary Magdalene, (Feast Day July 22) St. Dismas (Feast Day March 25) & St. Callistus (Feast Day October 14)— whose lives dramatically furthered and marked the course of the early Church.

Christ speaks powerfully to us in the manner of his death and whom he chose to accompany him and in his resurrection, whom he chose to first appear, both redeemed criminals; St. Dismas, the good thief and St. Mary Magdalene, the prostitute with pure heart.

III-2) For centuries Mary's conversion from prostitute to saint is continually being pulled away from her, and Dismas' feast day is not even celebrated, nor is Callistus remembered; as a Church built on a mission to sinners often tries to remove sinners from its past and presents a thief of pears as a great story of criminal conversion, but as great as St. Augustine was, he never walked where the deep sinners did.

Jesus Christ, the criminal, and the Catholic Church form a triptych held together by love, informed by charity, and realized by suffering.

Christ's mission was to the sinner and one of his central teachings was to teach the truth to the Pharisees, yet they called for his death, plotting with Judas to deliver him to the Roman governor Pilate for execution.

And if Christ himself could not teach the Pharisees, whose prophecy he fulfilled the truth of, who are we to think we can. No, they are who we must always struggle with, and whose actions will cause suffering among the people as they struggle to impose obedience.

The pharisaic conscience—which turns virtue into vice—is always among us, and the Pharisees who delivered Christ to crucifixion merely served as the paradigm setting agents in Jerusalem who began a process of denial and oppression of the Church which continues today, and whose origin is the prince of the world.

III-3) Criminalized and executed himself, Christ's first act of canonization was making the penitential criminal Dismas a saint, and upon his resurrection the first person to whom he revealed himself was the penitential criminal Mary Magdalene, the apostle to the apostles.

Dismas is the only human being to accompany the Lord in death, from earth to heaven—his partner in act one of the eternal three act drama central to human history—Christ has died, Christ has risen, Christ will come again.

Christ could have merely said, for the kind comment of Dismas; "Your sins are forgiven you", or "You will receive your reward in heaven" or any number of promises he had previously made in his ministry on earth, but he chose instead the greatest gift he ever gave to one sinner "Truly, I say to you, today you will be with me in Paradise."

To the criminal, to the thief Dismas, that is what our Lord said. And we must ask why? But we already know why, he came for the criminals, the deepest sinners of all, and for those penitential and redeemed criminals, they will be with him in paradise.

The joy of living God's law comes from choosing to live it and the deepest joy comes to those whose living of it has been a return and rebirth from the deepest sin.

III-4) Some biblical scholars have attempted to make a case that Mary Magdalene was not the prostitute legend says she was, but the stronger case is that she was; and it comes, not from critical biblical scholarship, but from an understanding of the transformed criminal, which she also certainly was.

The courage shown by Mary during the crucifixion and resurrection—and perhaps one of the reasons she is often called the apostle to the apostles—in the face of a threat great enough to send most of the other apostles into flight, is similar to that shown by Dismas the Good Thief, who even on the cross of crucifixion he shared next to Christ, had the courage to stand for truth and for Christ, rewarded by becoming the first canonized saint of the Church.

Great sinners who have become transformed into saints often bring with them a physical courage usually deeper than that of other saints (one can not imagine Mary Magdalene denying Christ three times as did Peter); and it springs from a personal experiential knowledge of evil, from which they no longer feel fear, but transcendence.

What magnificent joy was birthed within the penitential Mary Magdalene as Christ drove the devils from her, saving her from her criminal life; and what greater joy became hers as she came alone to the tomb and saw the risen Christ.

What magnificent joy befell Dismas as he went from the criminal cross to Christ's heavenly home, the home which all seek and to which all spurs to sanctification and perfection lead.

St. Dismas and St. Mary Magdalene are the proto-criminal saints, canonical consorts—first to heaven with Christ, first to see Christ arisen.

III-5) St. Callistus I, pope from 218-223, who was born a slave, became a thief, was sentenced to prison, escaped, transformed himself and became pope.

St. Callistus greatest contribution to the Church was during the time when the strictest among its leaders had succeeded in disallowing any return to the Church once having sinned. Callistus, having transformed himself so dramatically, would have none of this and allowed sinners, once having done penance, to return to the Church.

He established the practice of the absolution of all repented sins, against which much of the leadership of the Church at that time fought him, every step of the way, and gained him such strong enmity among the pharisaic members of the leadership that one of them, Hippolytus, set himself up—through an election of his supporters—as the anti-pope in response to Callistus and wrote scathingly against him for years.

Later, Hippolytus was also sent to prison and while there, discovered what Callistus had learned; that even with deep sin, redemption is offered. That is the essential message of the Lord, why Mary Magdalene was prophet to the prophets, Dismas the first canonized saint of the Church, and Callistus one of the greatest popes of the early Church.

For these three, it was their penitential criminality which canonized them.

Bended Knee

The call is not to obey Christ; the call is to be like Christ.

III-6) It has been said that the devil has very thin limbs with no knees, and not being able to kneel is the animating aspect of his evil.

Professional criminals resist bending to another's will, even God's, and this resistance is partly defiance and partly acknowledgement of the liberating power of freedom from influence.

III-7) Much of the drive to criminality is a drive for freedom, freedom from a world often seeking to oppress, seeking to deny, seeking to punish; yet it is this world the criminal seeks to avoid and thwart as he finds the criminal path—always leading into and through the great prison houses of history, the maximum security cells from which little light shines but that from internal liberty—and enters fully into the criminal world with its ancient rituals and laws; its crushing steel, stone, bone, and blood; and the loss of fear and the joy of power over destiny.

This is the martyr's freedom, the martyr's path, and in the lives of the great sinner saints, the criminals, the prodigal sons; St. Mary Magdalene the prostitute who became the apostle to the apostles; St. Dismas, the good thief who became the first canonized saint of the Church; St. Callistus, the criminal who became pope; St Augustine, the thief who became a father of the Church; St. John of the Cross, who within a prison cell wrote of the great ascension of the spirit to meet God; and all of the other deep sinners and criminals who, knowing evil, became more deeply good.

III-8) We seek the blessings of those who found within the mysteries of the Church the simple truths of Christ and eternity, yet remained awhirl with the majesty of the accumulated knowledge of her saints— especially those of her criminal saints— whose deep knowledge led them to the Roman road.

III-9) It is a mistake to equate the theological position of obeisance (deferential respect) to God with obedience (doing what one is told), as the great call to perfection is not to do what one is told but to be what one truly is; a human being made in the image of God, whose earthly sin has been redeemed by Christ and whose promise is to fulfill perfection of life on this earth and bringing other souls to Christ through the daily work on that path of perfection.

The call is not to obey Christ; the call is to be like Christ.

And the most powerful attribute of man from God is his free will, which led him to eat of the fruit of the tree of knowledge— the tree of life; and this is perhaps where we see the sin of Satan, that he wanted to force man to do good, where God gifted freedom of action.

This is perhaps most evident in the book of Job where God allows Satan to punish the good man with all manner of evils to forcefully influence Job's free will to decide to respond to evil with evil; yet Job does not and continues to praise the Lord

Children of Eve

Eve is the mother of us all as Mary is the Mother of the Church; one leads us to our free will and the great danger in exercising it and the other leads us to eternal salvation through her Son.

III-10) Criminals are, like Eve, those who say no to God's plan and yes to the serpent promising knowledge, power, and freedom, but they must learn to become children of Mary and live her divine yes.

The children of Eve love the pleasures of the world, love the hopes for secret knowledge and power that is assumed to come from a deeper tasting of them—often true, so true—yet in their relentless searching find that the way of delight is a path to sadness.

III-11) The criminal bears his cross with the Church; like St. Dismas, he deserves to be here, hanging on Golgotha; like St. Mary Magdalene, he deserves shame and a lifetime of penance; like St. Pope Callistus, he knows human redemption because he exemplifies it.

III-12) The bad is good. The bad, seeing itself as bad, becomes good. Only the sinner can become a saint. The merely good is a voice of no timbre, no octaval range or depth.

III-13) The good from the present evil in the Church of priests sexually abusing children and the bishops who countenanced it, is the reminder that, for as long as the Church has existed, the smoke and fire of Satan can enter into the hearts of its priests, bishops, and even its popes; but the Church will not fall, even unto the gates of Hell.

III-14) Eve birthed a world through her succumbing to the great temptation to know, to become, and as we seek becoming through the exploration of the bad, let us find on the other side of it, the truly good.

Eve is the mother of us all as Mary is the Mother of the Church; one leads us to our free will and the great danger in exercising it, and the other leads us to eternal salvation through her Son.

IV- Part Two
The Cross

The cross you are to bear is what you are here to do, at that point when you discover that the most important thing to do is to take on your cross and shoulder the courage of Christ and all the saints.

The Great Story

The great story remains unfinished, yet God created us, in his image, for life in the eternal garden of the newly created earth, radiant with glorious life, beauty, and joy; but we failed him.

IV-1) 𝔚e cannot know the mind of God, but we can use the gifts from his word and image—our reason and our being—and embracing the reality of the deep knowledge we have acquired through our experience, our work in the academy, our professional training, our study of the social teaching of the Catholic Church, all animated by our sacramental Catholicism; connect with the substantive reality of the natural law, forming a union with our self as God's child, and come to comprehend, in a most elemental way, the pattern of his work.

In this way, let us look at the great story of our kind upon the earth, and beyond it, to see what has perhaps been revealed to us through the actions of God's work.

God created the first human being in his own image—he created us in his image—think of that, think of that divine birth heritage, reaching back from each of us to the first man, to the adamic core.

As he shaped Adam from that primordial dust, as into his face he wove the divine features into the first man, and as he is spiritual, he imparted to us eternal spirit and as spiritual beings, possessing a central spiritual asset, free will—thus God was giving up any control over human action save persuasion—and he established the first part of the old covenant with Adam.

There is only one concrete material way we can know of the truth of this creation; through the works of God can we know of the existence of God. Through the truths he has written on our heart; yet to discover these the criminal must search deep and long and return again to the halls of study and the bench of prayer; for, as criminals, we resist the imposition of any truth but that we learn for ourselves, that we see for ourselves, that we experience for ourselves.

Exercising their free will, human beings embraced the evil—hidden in an appeal to their emerging vision of self—emanating from the persuasive words of Satan, the fallen angel whose free willed choice removed him from God forever with absolutely no chance for redemption.

Satan, and the angels who rejected God, with full knowledge of God, as created angelic beings of God, can never—on account of their irrevocable rejection of the Creator—find forgiveness; yet the greatest criminal can, even the most evil of criminals can; and though it may be with the bloody spur of approaching death from the execution by a state no longer able to protect the innocent against the criminal aggressor any other way than through his death; here still the salvation can come, the forgiveness can come.

This eternal forgiveness can only be found from God, and he has, through his divine authority, given the ability to his priests, working in concert with and from within the Church he founded upon earth, that those who sin can, by confession and penance, receive forgiveness and begin again with their life, renewed.

For thousands of years human beings practiced their evil upon the earth and most wickedly within its cities; cities founded by the darkest of the proto human evil-doers, Cain, where the city crowds acted in their lives downward to the lure of Satan rather than upward to the call of God.

This pagan world became so intolerable and such an assault upon the face of God that he flooded the earth, removing all humans, animals, and cities; save those in the great ark, and with its helmsman Noah, God created the second part of the old covenant.

God established the third covenant with Abraham, the first man to have his name changed by God, as Abraham was to create the People of God, the Jews, and as the father of nations the prophecy of the creation of the Kingdom of God to be brought by Christ was foretold.

For the generations of Abraham, and then from the great exodus from Egypt, God worked through Moses to build up the

People of God, wrote the commandments they were to live by with his own hand and the laws governing their behavior with his own voice, and with Moses and the Jews God created the third and final part of the old covenant, the Sinai Covenant.

For thousands of years the People of God struggled to live as God's People, fought against the admonishments of their prophets, and they failed him again. This brought him to earth as a human being, becoming that which was made in his father's image, becoming the man God Jesus Christ, and walking among the People of God, he grew to manhood and for three years God taught his people directly, sealing his teaching with the universality of his Church under the New Covenant, and established his Church with Peter, upon whose rock of heart he expanded the People of God to include all who would hear the word, the word that became flesh.

Catholics are bound to the Jews—as the Jews are God's chosen people—and we are bound to the Jews as we are the people who chose God.

Christ built his church upon Peter, who had thrice denied him, and throughout the history of the Church would deny him again, but the marriage between God and Church would stand, through better or worse, as it had with his chosen people.

IV-2) The drawings of St. John of the Cross, particularly of the ascent of the mount—the interiority of the great story— are so like those we see by prisoners in super-max, incredibly detailed, spiritual praxis.

IV-3) The beauty of the great story is that we already know the ending, we already know how it comes out, yet each day is still a test of our faith in that knowing, against the deadly and powerful allure of the temporal world and reaching to the still small voice of the eternal as we can hear it now.

IV-4) God told the great story to humans many times, through prophets mostly, but it was ignored, then finally he came himself to tell it, to show it, to live it, and yet, it was still largely ignored, but for the Church he left behind, invested still with his life daily—though still largely ignored—even by his Church who counts angels upon needles and wonders if conception is really the beginning of human life.

The great story remains unfinished, yet God created us, in his image, for life in the eternal garden of the newly created earth, radiant with glorious life, beauty, and joy; but we failed him.

He called from among us, from among the dark pagan world, a people chosen to bring us all too eternal life, but they failed him.

He came among his himself, teaching with his divine power and living his human life and finally the truth came to earth and stayed, built upon the rock of Peter, restoring us still.

Evil in the World

Satan's involvement in evil has been clearly stated by the Church since the beginning and remains so.

IV-5) The churning and turning of demographic trends due to some catastrophe or generational evil is as ancient as the earth and they will always continue as the prince of the world works his ways and we fall prey to them again and again.

Some scholars look at the demographics of prisons and conclude that the fact of a disproportionate number being ethnic minorities defines the system as corrupt; while criminals know that the demographics only portray the increased opportunity to become a criminal in an environment where so many already have chosen the exciting and remunerative path to success criminality represents.

Our hope is always in the Lord and in his Church and in our own hearts yearning for freedom and eternal life, and we will endure till the end of time, for the war has already been won by Christ Jesus, though we still fight the battles of the cross every day.

IV-6) Satan's involvement in evil has been clearly stated by the Church since the beginning and remains so.

Satan, after being thrown from heaven and falling to the world, was allowed to be the prince of this world, bringing evil into it, realized through the original temptation of Eve and the proto murder of Abel, but with the coming of Christ he was conquered.

It is in the Book of Job that we see the interaction between God and Satan around the human will, which Satan wants to destroy, and his sin that had him cast from heaven; which I think is that Satan wanted the humans to be forced to be good but God gave us free will, reflecting his nature and that of all heaven.

What is a wonder is not that evil runs rampant in the world, but that good still triumphs, not that criminals shape the culture of the world, but that saints subdue it, not that we are always tempted by it, but that we mostly resist it, not that we give in to it, but that we seek redemption when we do.

The perfect world for the predator is a world without protection for the innocent—states unwilling to declare war or use capital punishment—a world where there is literally no sin, all is relative; and if you do not know what prince of the world is behind this way of thinking, you do not *know*.

IV-7) There are those who have thought that the route to good, to saintliness, to enlightenment, is through the path of evil, coming to intimately know its shadow life and sensual reality to break through its tempting power to reach the Holy Grail.

There are those who have traveled this path and have learned, after deep sojourns into the criminal world of evil, that the suffering coming from the resulting soul scarring and the depth of knowledge learned in those dark paths is certainly most valuable—though not necessarily in the pursuit of saintliness—but in the teaching of others discovering the eternal terror that lies in the future of one continuing down that path, and it is surely down...deeply down.

You cannot know evil by seeing it, by fighting it, by containing it, but only by doing it; for it is first being, then comes knowing.

If you don't know the power of evil, it is difficult to choose, with conviction, the greater power of good, which has to be known, not surmised.

IV-8) The value of evil is the value of the good that can come from it, and the weapon those surviving evil unto redemption have to help those still caught by it—is a fiery sword wielded directly against Satan—and through the words of Catholic social teaching and the deep sharpening of daily suiting up in the armor of God, giving holy fire to its blade, creating the fiery sword through which souls can be saved.

IV-9) Traditional rehabilitative programs for criminals rely on providing service to address specific needs the reentering criminal has, and it is in this very connection (service to need) that the larger truth of criminality is over-looked.

Criminality, in its professional sense, is chosen, and the choice comes from an internal array of experience that sees no or little value—other than when sanctioned— to choose another way.

IV-10) Somewhere around the middle of the 20th Century, Catholics quit talking about evil and Satan grew stronger.

Oh indeed, the scattered pieces of the great Church still murmured a bit about evil and Satan, but they had no weapons against it, so what did it matter?

And most of the Catholic priests were long ago silent with only Peter able to still see its markings clear.

IV-11) Wars are as much a part of human history as crime and violence and the attempts by the historical unwary to develop a pattern of thinking and behavior that they assume will result in world peace are not the best way to spend one's time, for the kingdom of heaven is not of this world.

A characteristic that appears to be present in the folks who spend their time resisting those social institutions in our country that are largely operating under the mantle of our society's responsibility to protect — whether their resistance involves working to shut down military installations, ban capital punishment, or release most criminals from prison—is a clear unawareness of the reality of evil, and for Catholics, who have at their fingertips, within the deep well of the magisterium, the most developed intellectual and spiritual resources concerning the work of the prince of this world available anywhere, that is inexcusable.

So often heresy occurs when dissenters try to create absolutes when contingency is needed, and create contingency when absolutes are needed; or they just go backwards.

IV-12) Christ needed Dismas—who had protected him before—and more than a few criminals had a good heart as did Dismas.

And I have dreamt that God, promising that the gates of hell would not prevail, created the Order of Dismas, knights from the gates to ensure they were closed about the Church, the Order of the Good Thief keeping the underworld from being an open door to the gates of hell.

After Christ's crucifixion, when he took Dismas with him to hell, but returned three days later in his resurrection, he left Dismas in hell, the criminal saint strong enough to save criminal souls.

The order is the final bulwark of redemption.

Super max was tough time, but peaceful, time enough to contemplate the vision from St. Dismas, of an underworld where resistance to the evil one was as strong as the submission, and it was only from us, penitential professional criminals—with transformed hearts and deeply armored with daily communion with God—yet familiar with the darkest joys of the criminal world and the deepest pits of the carceral, but with the strength of spirit to defy the will of the evil one in his natural home.

IV-13) God allows evil to exist because we must have the choice to choose evil, otherwise what value is free will if the world is only good.

As we do this and as we reflect upon our doing, we see how important justice is to our work, how important that profit not drive our activity—harming the souls of transforming criminals and their potential and opportunities for life and happiness— but adding to that, growing it as the soundest profit of all.

Reflection and prayer, so necessary to the capitalist, to the professional, to the public servant, to the apostolate so that power so widely wielded may not harm another but always help.

In the economic arena where so much has gone wrong for so long and where the deception of liberation theology and its denying God as redemptive source and claiming Marxism as the way, led so many of the faithful astray—still so.

Sinai and Golgotha have forged the great link of solidarity between old and new, forged in those three days and blood seals.

Sinners become saints, and transformed criminals warring against evil, carry heavy armor into that war, deep scars of the internal battles waged in the steel and stone of prisons and the candelabra streets of the city nights.

Yet we wander in our helping ways often blindly, we follow where we do not know, we are called and we must go, each day, each enraged and evil soul to calm and transform. It is why we are here, it is what we are made to be, what we are made to do. As the Sabbath is traditionally consecrated for good works, those whose work is an apostolate of transforming criminals, consecrate every day to it. How do we consecrate ourselves to continually receive the grace that underlies the power of good works, to continually struggle against the indifference of others, the suffering that deadens the will to grow, and the pain that stifles the spirit?

C.S. Lewis said that the greatest success of the devil was to have convinced people he didn't exist, but we have seen his works and we know that he exists.

Having once embraced evil but then awakening through the Church and God's grace, seeing and grasping the light, beginning the transformative process, walking again as a child in the sunlight, resolutely finding our way, until we know that our work has only just begun, that now it is the criminals still among us that we must help.

We are armed with the cruel hardness of our experience and the sharp edge of our salvation and the knowledge of walking in the light.

We were lost and now we are found, who but to us does the battle fall?

Life in the World

God is the fount of our perfection and provides the grace for the path but we are the instrument upon which the symphony of Christ's sacrifice is universalized.

IV-14) Life is eternal life—which must be our only horizon in our daily life—and that of the world is the ground where we determine where our eternal life shall be lived, in heaven or hell.

The desert fathers felt their choice of life in the desert would put them on a ground of less temptation, thereby bringing them closer to an eternal heavenly life, and their prayers and powerful spiritual development did that, while blessing all others to whom their prayers were offered.

Our time on earth is choosing eternity—either of fire and pain or warmth and joy—it is as if we are preparing for the day, choosing what we will wear and from our closet take the garments we'll wear forevermore—that brief moment at our closet door is an eternity compared to real eternal time and the life we choose therein from our work in the world.

IV-15) Christ drove the moneychangers from the temple because they reversed the natural order of things; for it is the reality of the temple that should flow out into the world, not the reality of the world into the temple.

The priests had given away their calling and became part of the world, and it was this which called forth God's personal anger and its physical manifestations; as he would today if he was upon the earth in human form and entered the Church, and saw the great filth there from which Peter draws such shame, and from where he, Christ Jesus, would whip the pedophile priests and the bishops who moved them around like chess pieces, into the dark night and the deep ocean which they had called upon themselves, sinking with the great millstone about their necks, pulling them down into the hell they had created in the hearts of the little ones.

IV-16) The world values the cold, calculating, bureaucratic precision that can dispatch life and treasure in pursuit of an organizational imperative with emotional and moral impunity and this calculus is woven into criminal world choices where death, maiming, or prison awaits failure.

IV-17) How often we forget, in our fear of Satan as prince of this world, that our call to the apostolate is a call to always advance the world towards the Kingdom of Heaven the world is always, inexorably, becoming.

In this sense, the basic thread of liberation theology—faith without works is dead—is correct, merely writ large for our time in that place of tyrants.

IV-18) There is no war between good and evil in the world, because God triumphed on the cross, but there is always one in the human soul struggling against the lies of Satan; which we effectively armor ourselves against by continual praying, the every day practice of Mass, morning prayers, communion, midday prayers, praying the rosary, examination of conscience, resolutions, evening prayers, sacrifices and mortification—this daily practice renders the battle won when done with a humble heart, courageous will, and joyous soul.

IV-19) As the solution for labor is the union, the solution to crime is the criminal.

IV-20) The great and constant call from the Church to serve God is not as much about service as it is about humility for us—a creature too often assuming we 'are as gods'—and while serving others as if they are God/Christ is a cross lightly borne.

Each of us is an instrument in the great symphony of the Kingdom of Heaven where the Trinity conducts, and our task is to learn to read the music, determining our places, our rhythm and rhyme; taking the Good News to whom God has called us to serve.

IV-21) Learning about the great heresies, starting with the book of the same name by H. Belloc, will define the enemies of the Church in this world and help us—along with our work helping one another—help the Church in her eternal struggle against them.

The greatest heresy, whose spread was by the sword, will only be defeated by the sword and it is not to the soft Catholics that chore falls, but to the hard, the men of steel and stone, the men whose transformation from evil to good has not removed their ability to fight with the blade.

IV-22) Being involved in the politics of the time is crucial, to not only remain aware of the signs of the times, but to be able to support those political movements and leaders who best represent Catholic social teaching.

IV-23) A great charge to us is to better our world, to be useful and to serve; to create more abundance for our fellow human beings, to care for and nourish the ground upon which we stand together by being gardeners of the soil of human fulfillment, to be just and loving in our dealings with others, and to always stand on truth, our final and greatest friend, guided by the loving hands of God.

Being friends with the truth embedded in Catholic social teaching is to *"Go with Peter, to Christ, through Mary"*, the guiding principle arching over the truth of the teaching, wedded to scripture through tradition and centuries of reflection.

Through this lens, and through this practice, the social teaching makes its way into our lives, embroidered and filled out through the papal encyclicals, a clear trajectory of correct practice informing us now.

Being friends with truth is in knowing the absolute centrality of human beings within creation, in knowing innocent life absolutely must be protected, in knowing all things are possible through God and even the darkest soul can discover the light.

Then, here is our ultimate friend, this truth we seek and for which, in this complex and modern world where appearance shades reality, calls us to even deeper searching.

He awaits our call for guidance; whose word has guided the millennia guides us still, as prevalent now and as fresh as when written on ancient parchment in ancient times, but a breath in God's mystery for us.

He has died, He is Risen, He shall come again.

V-Part Three
The Church

Real time is eternal time, and real religion—the theology of the real—is built upon it. False time is human time and false religion is built upon it.

Life in the Church

Today we can visit with Peter each day, and from his comings and goings draw solace and truth to armor us in our communion path.

V-1) The architecture of the Church, from ancient times, reflects the embrace of God, who is represented in the Tridentine Mass by the People of God facing Him who embraces them as they embrace Him, while the new mass confuses still as the embrace often seems to be the people embracing the priest, the priest embracing the people, and God floats behind the priest, watching; and in front of the people, waiting.

The ancient material architecture reinforces the spiritual architecture, from a point above to the people below, the great hierarchy moves through space and time, creating a holy cathedral of our sacramental lives.

The ancient hierarchy is absolute as the truth is absolute and together they embody the material and spiritual architecture.

V-2) Christ made the covenant with Peter and the People of God: "And I say to thee: That thou art Peter; and upon this rock I will build my church, and the gates of hell shall not prevail against it." (Matthew 16: 18-19)

It is to Peter and the universal catechisms brought forth under his authority— *Catechism of the Council of Trent* under Pope Pius V and the *Catechism of the Catholic Church* under Pope John Paul II— that we need look for teaching authority as it is he who is the rock the Church is built upon.

The institutional church is a bureaucracy and that bureaucracy stretches from parish to the Vatican and by its nature— governance by the interiority of bureaucracies, so tragically seen during the sexual abuse crisis in the Untied States—is easily corrupted and seeking teaching authority from it can lead us astray, while Peter will not.

In this time of the internet we are fortunate to have at our fingertips access to the Vatican and Peter and it is a simple matter to refresh ourselves at the Rock as often as needed.

Today we can visit with Peter each day, and from his comings and goings draw solace and truth to armor us in our communion path.

V-3) Much of the life in the Church is dealing with the continual attacks by Satan on the Church, so often embedded in the frothy language of crowd appeal or directed toward human pride, the various ideologies that attempt to destroy the Church over the past few centuries range from those of socialism, relativism, new age religions, ecological spirituality, but all come from the ancient revolt of Gnosticism, that the truth is held by secret, by initiates, by an elite who can share bits and pieces of it with the common folk, but the folk cannot reach the depth and breadth of it alone.

Revealed truth is housed openly in the Church and the more deeply we study its precepts, the more joyful we become, as it continues to unfold itself before our eyes, resonating within our heart and mind and spirit.

V-4) To the Buddhist, suffering cannot be stopped, all one can do it detach from it, indeed that is the best one can do.

To the Catholic, suffering can be transformed into exaltation.

V-5) The criminal, having rejected religion—civic, pagan, monotheistic—is essentially a nihilist, but can, through the carceral experience, find remorse and seek penance.

To the penitential criminal, the work that will be effective in the transformation of criminals will come from the grassroots community organizations developed and led by penitential and transformed criminals, who are deep knowledge leaders of efforts that have much in common with those that proved successful working with the poor through small groups in Latin America as part of the Liberation Theology movement.

To the institutional Catholic Church we would ask if the preferential option for the poor applies to penitential criminals?

Does this describe criminals? No and yes. No, while they are still active criminals because they wait for nothing, as do the poor, but take what they want, and rather than often being robbed by unjust laws, as are the poor, it is they who rob the innocent.

But yes, as penitential criminals, they become statistics, and stand before the halls of society waiting for admittance which never comes, and they are forevermore excluded.

The need for the Church within the criminal world is great now, as prisons— the universities and cathedrals of crime— have grown so massive that their underworld is shaping upperworld to a degree not seen since the darkest days of paganism, when Christ was compelled to come.

In the saying yes to the prince of this world, the criminal learns the ways of the predator, and becoming predators, have reason to be aware of the habits of their prey—who rarely know they are such—thus feeling no reason to become as they are.

In this sense, in most encounters between the two—particularly within the traditional rehabilitative field—the predator usually triumphs.

V-6) The Catholic Church in America is, as it pertains to coherent institutional support for the magisterium, in lax condition. As a result of many factors, but culminating in the sexual abuse tragedy, which itself is part of a larger loss of faith by the American bishops and priests, the points of interaction within the public square—almost all within the arena of the Church's social teaching—have almost all been dictated by the secular world.

Whether it involves the issues—abortion, euthanasia, capital punishment or war—the American institutional Church has virtually become the handmaid of the world rather than the bride of Christ, and the innocent faithful have paid the most horrific price as they, their families, and their parish communities have been corrosively degraded by corrupt priests and bishops.

Yet, among the ruins, the promise of our Lord that the gates of hell shall not prevail, must give us strength—the innocent faithful, the steadfast bishops and priests—

to continue to speak out through the great apostolate work in protection of Christ's bride.

"With Peter, to Christ, through Mary, for the Greater Glory of God"

V-7) The Church existed before creation, the divine dream of a communion with God and human freely entered into from a world where the divine is rarely evident and evil is the rule of the world. Satan is its prince and humans are like Job scourged by devils at fever pitch, yet in that earthly fire and sensual passion remains, after discovering it—a true holding to the still small voice of love—a true holding to God— a true holding to the eternal Church.

Honor has been largely lost in the world, largely lost in the priests of the Church, but it still reigns in the hearts of men of good will, with Peter and the teaching of the Church.

The clerical sexual abuse is incest as the celibate bound fathers who seduce the faithful are seducing their children, the children of the family of the Church.

V-8) The theologians are too often politicians and it takes the professional amateurs like Belloc or Chesterton to speak the truth clearly, again reinforcing the apostolate of the laity.

V-9) It is not about obedience, but love of our birthright of divinity, of our divine connection to our creator as his adopted sons and daughters.

Obedience is what Satan proposes, obedience to sin and it is for slaves; love is God's hope and it is for saints, angels, and human beings.

It begins by helping the stranger, being the Good Samaritan, who saw not a member of an enemy tribe but a human being. Before Christ, among tribal cultures, strangers were enemies. His teaching of praying for our enemy was a profound idea and still is. Witness Pope John Paul II visiting the man who attempted to assassinate him and forgiving him, witness the Vatican's plea that Saddam Hussein, soon after being captured and photographed disheveled and dirty in the hospital where he was taken, be treated with dignity and respect.

Loving our neighbors and praying for our enemies can only be done freely. Grassroots nonprofits help freely and donors support them freely. It is the best arrangement and congruent with the principle of subsidiarity. In this way the role of government is to act as a facilitator of technical and financial resources to help grassroots organizations, who have the embedded community expertise, to do the work of personal transformation.

The social doctrine of the Catholic Church revolves about this interaction of one person with another, with preference for the poor, the marginal, the suffering. This essential human relationship with one another and with our Creator is where our work of transformation begins and ends.

Capital Punishment

In the Great Commandment we have the whole of the Law, which cannot be changed; and love of neighbor means protecting the innocent against the aggressor; the divine justification of capital punishment and just war.

V-10) **C**apital punishment is a central aspect of the social teaching of the Church in relation to the work of the Lampstand Foundation in the transformation of criminals, as it is the ultimate criminal sanction, and has been since ancient times a bulwark of the teaching of the Church regarding the protection of the innocent against the aggressor. One of the strongest statements from Christ concerning capital punishment is Matthew 18:6; "Whoever causes one of these little ones who believe in me to sin, it would be better for him to have a great millstone fastened round his neck and to be drowned in the depth of the sea."

Saint Augustine, St. Thomas Aquinas, the Catechism of the Council of Trent and the current Catechism, all continued that support.

The strength of the social teaching to transform criminals is in its eternal congruence—what was always true is true still—and God clearly mandated capital punishment as a just response to deep evil under the old covenant, which nothing in the new covenant countermanded, regardless of the attempts to do so under some ill-defined spirit of the age argument which, even in its proffering, cuts at the rock of traditional truth.

V-11) Capital punishment is a rooted part of the Church's long advocated protection of the innocent against the aggressor, whether through the abortion and euthanasia prohibition or the principles of just war.

It is a central element in the responsibility to protect—embraced by the prayer given to us, the *Our Father*—and carried forward into time by Peter.

The deep wonder is that Peter, though he may even be a sinful man, cannot destroy the Church, for Christ promised its survival, even unto the gates of hell.

V-12) Politics and public policy—and how they blend—has been difficult for the Catholic faithful for years, and the issues surrounding the political factions of the Catholic Church in the United States— generally divided by the level of congruence to the magisterium on the issue of abortion—are explored.

The documents of the magisterium, because they have been written for the Church Universal are couched in intellectually subtle terms that are widely embracing, while still revealing to the attentive reader the narrow path.

Consequently, the documents can often lend encouragement to those who find support to conflate being against capital punishment (which the Church is not) to being against abortion (which the Church is).

V-13) Recently there has emerged a call for an end to the use of capital punishment—based primarily on statements by Pope John Paul II—when other means can be used to protect the innocent from the aggressor, but this call has been built on a lack of understanding of the Catholic historic record regarding criminal justice issues and the understanding among criminal justice professionals that even within the confines of a maximum security prison, criminals are still able to influence aggression against the innocent.

Those calling for this are often handicapped in presenting a proper analysis of criminal justice, as can be seen in their failure to properly understand the hard reality of the deep involvement of Satan in the criminal world, and could it be any more obvious that within the darkest bowels of our nation's prisons the animating visage is that of the devil.

Too many fail to face Satan and his works, but excuse away and become mere apologists for criminal behavior, rather than realizing it for what it often is, the work of the devil; and thus does he continue his greatest deception, of continuing the lie that he does not even exist.

Not knowing the lengths bad people will go to in pursuit of evil has long plagued the perspective of people of good will. However, it is a fundamental strength of the perspective of reformed criminals with a long sojourn in the criminal world and maximum security prisons to not be so plagued.

This great difficulty in experientially understanding the darkness of evil, motivates the intentions of Catholics, whose traditional teaching has provided them the intellectual information and spiritual tools capable of countering it, who nevertheless, wish to abolish capital punishment.

In the struggle between good and evil the world only wins by its own values, but in eternal time the good triumphed long ago, and in the perspective we bring to the importance of retaining the option of capital punishment, we need to see the horizon of eternity and the knowledge of hell.

One of the portals Satan seeks to enter to weaken the Church is that of protecting the innocent life, and unfortunately, he often is helped by Catholics who do not understand the connection between the traditional support of the Church for capital punishment and its traditional censure of abortion.

By conflating life issues such as abortion, euthanasia, war, and capital punishment, they conflate the innocence of the pre-born, the elderly, and disabled, with the evil of the aggressor who has destroyed innocent life and has been justly condemned by lawful civil authorities, rendering unto Caesar which is his.

Banning capital punishment could very well be a stalking horse for approving abortion.

The weakening of the social prohibition of abortion also weakens that of murder to the point even the progressively self-defined members of the Catholic Church justify nothing any longer calls for the ultimate punishment; a tradition that is as ancient as the church.

If the abolition of capital punishment succeeds, the responsibility of the evil doer to suffer punishment befitting the evil done, and the opportunity to be saved from the eternal torments of hell, has also been lost, and the further step of removing personal responsibility from those who commit the evil of abortion, euthanasia, and unjust war, begins to lose its moral standing.

Those within the social science field, informed by Catholic teaching and with a professional knowledge of criminal justice issues and a deeper understanding of the hand of Satan within the criminal world, are clearer in their development of the doctrine.

The Church's traditional support for capital punishment—validated in Catholic teaching for millennia—is based on the assumption of the reality of evil (which the relativist thinking secular world, clearly influencing the Church in the West, struggles to accept) that some offenses are so terrible that the only just and charitable response is to consign the evil doer to hell, and hope that within that definite period of earthly life he now knows, after sentenced to death, remains to him, he will be spurred to seek forgiveness.

V-14) The transition from traditional documents to new isn't one of languishing support for capital punishment but of language, and it is more sadly held as a regrettable aspect of human and Church history that none find joy or glory in its promotion.

The difference between the old *Roman Catechism*, the first edition of the current *Catechism* and the second edition of the current *Catechism of the Catholic Church* reflects modern language sensitivity—part of the modernist, relativist age we live in and not all bad—that treats difficult subjects with a subtle deference to compassion for the inevitability of our sin; but there has been no change in doctrine, nor the traditional support of the Church for capital punishment.

The proper response to evil is punishment—appropriately found in Hell—and capital punishment speeds that consequence while human mercy delays God's judgment, so clearly stated by Christ with the millstone statement in Matthew.

V-15) During the period of the 1960's through the 1980's, certain religious orders, cardinals, bishops, and priests of the Catholic Church—particularly in the

Americas—became enamored of the Marxist-inspired Liberation Theology and informed by its anti-capitalism, absorbed the corresponding attributes of restricting the power of capitalistic countries, including their legal and military power, resulting in strong anti-war and anti-capital punishment movements.

This perspective bled into the arguments incorporated in the formation of the current catechism, watering down, particularly in those two areas, the historic clarity the Catholic Church had presented to the world regarding capital punishment.

As the Church now beats back the minor degradation of Church doctrine influenced by Liberation Theology—a battle still joined—the clarity should return, particularly around the issues of protecting the life of the innocent through the just use of war and capital punishment.

There are many reasons for concern in this 'language sensitivity', chief being the relative lack of knowledge of criminal justice issues, in the claim that the super-max prison can forever restrain the aggressor, yet those in the criminal justice field know how easily the imprisoned aggressor—even within super-max or death row—can act against those innocents outside of prison.

When we add to this language sensitivity, the terrible disruption of the sexual scandal the Church began experiencing during that period, though not becoming public until much later, the unraveling of even the settled language, and the rearrangement of the dogmatic expression emanating from the Second Vatican Council, it is a wonder that as much of the hard truths that sustained the Church for the millennia, survived as strongly expressed as they have.

And this confusion was only compounded by the lack of leadership, resulting from the corruption of the sexual scandal, of those most responsible for providing teaching to the Church around the social teaching issues.

Along with this degraded leadership, another weakness in the United States Catholic approach to capital punishment and other criminal justice issues is—as mentioned—a lack of professional knowledge from the field and an understanding of the Church's historic work around punishment and prisons.

Recently however, there are encouraging developments for a deeper understanding of criminal justice, social science, and Catholic historic contributions to it.

V-16) It is from the examination of protecting society from convicted criminals that we consider the proper use of capital punishment as a legitimate sanction for serial pedophiles and serial rapists.

There is an aspect here that connects to the Just War doctrine, where it is the moral stance around the violence inherent in wars of many against many, where this addresses the violence within the war of the few against many and the many against the few.

V-17) Perhaps what is most marked about the position of the social teaching in the United States—and many others who study it—is the generally accepted assumption that the Church's work in this area began with the 1891 encyclical of Pope Leo XIII.

The difficulty with relying on this perception is that much of the foundational work of the social teaching—coming from the Old Testament and medieval sources—is not factored in, resulting in a skewed result.

This is particularly true with capital punishment, prisons, and punishment in general, which saw much of its most articulate principles developed during those periods, well documented by the work of Rodger Charles S.J. and Dr. Andrew Skotnicki.

With the publication of the United States Conference of Catholic Bishops *United States Catholic Catechism for Adults* in 2006, the Bishops validated their earlier statements that capital punishment "cannot be justified".

The divergence here is a reminder that we should look to the Bishop of Rome and the *Catechism* from the Vatican, for resolution when questions arise around interpretation.

V-18) For much of human history, the social value of human beings in the pagan world was barely above that of other objects, and this extreme devaluing of persons influenced the development of the practice around capital punishment.

With the moral development of the Judeo-Christian world the value of individual human beings increased and those of the innocent even more so, reflected by their protection in the law through the use of capital punishment.

V-19) In our reflections on the social teaching we want to use our historical perspective with a realization of the evolving nature of the teaching in relation to that of social development.

We see this played out in the teaching around capital punishment, as the Old Testament and the teachings of the medieval Fathers describe many occasions when it may be applied, yet it has developed such that today it is called for rarely.

The new language of the Church—while perhaps a bit sensitive—has the right pitch, expressing great compassion for the executed, as is proper, while clearly retaining the authority to execute, and this is congruent with the Church's thinking around the development of doctrine.

God was very clear in what he revealed, both at Sinai and soon after his transfiguration when he taught his disciples about scandal, that the death of the evil doer is often justified when the physical or spiritual life of the innocent is involved.

The entire tradition of the Church has always and continues to support the use of capital punishment, and yet, we should always use it carefully, compassionately, justly, and treating even the evil doer with the dignity and respect his humanity has received from God.

V-20) A proud moment for all Catholics was when the Vatican spoke out in defense of the Iraqi tyrant Saddam Hussein—when upon his arrest the pictures of him disheveled and in obvious distress were sent out to the world—asking that his human dignity and respect be observed by the authorities, regardless of what evil he had committed upon the innocent.

V-21) The protection of the innocent grounds respect for human life on four pillars; 1) Protecting babies within the womb—as Christ was protected within Mary's blessed womb—and it requires all legal action to the point of passing a constitutional amendment banning abortion. 2) Protecting the individual from the criminal aggressor, requiring all legal restraint to the point of taking the life of the aggressor if it is the only way to protect the innocent. 3) Protecting the nation from the criminal nation, requiring going to war to protect the nation from a direct threat, even if that threat is only verbal but comes from a nation possessing weapons of mass destruction. 4) Protecting the aged, sick, and disabled from euthanasia, requiring all legal restraint to the point of passing a constitutional amendment banning euthanasia.

V-22) What greater love for the deeply evil than to specify, through a date certain to the minute—of the ending of a ruinous life—so that redemption can be sought for the eternal salvation God promises to the penitential sinner.

But the state, with endless delays, reaching to the final minutes over and over again removes this certainty and allows Satan the final say as the evil doer resists the penance in the realistic hope of yet another delay.

V-23) We are bound, as Catholics, from the very beginning, to protect the innocent from the aggressor, and when he comes for the children, we are all holy knights of the cross, ready to lay down our life fighting for the children. When he, the aggressor, came in America, he was a prince and a priest of the Church and he ravished the children for years and we did nothing, and he still sits in the bishop's chair, and the great millstone awaits his passing and it will drag him into the deepest depth of the fire seas of hell.

So, as we come to the end of our journey through the 5th commandment, the great *not* in the Great Commandment of neighborly love, we know that for sound guidance and the final word, we must look to the Holy Father, we must look to the Holy See, we must look to the center, for truly, the center holds.

V-24) The adversary is eternally patient, knowing man's fallen nature eventually turns his way, and the human creature, rather than standing clearly in the revealed truth of the ancient revelation animating the Church, bends to the spirit of the times, embraces the world and loses site of eternity; loses sight that from time immemorial justice has demanded the gravest punishment for the gravest sin; and in the spirit of the age lends his human agency in the remorseless pulling of a foundation stone from the eternal tabernacle; giving the tiniest—but just enough—entrance to the slithering serpent.

Beyond Liberation Theology

Going beyond liberation theology is realizing that the only true liberation is from the greatest lie ever imagined to the greatest story ever told...

V-25) **W**hen I began, some time after my final release from prison in 1969, to examine the world and my life from the eyes of freedom, I did not know that I was still using my criminal mind—with its perspective that evil is relative—and embraced Marxism; which is profoundly evil and deeply criminal, as it represents a complete rejection of God, promoting the concept that man alone determines the ultimate reality and indeed, can create heaven on earth.

That concept entered the Church as liberation theology.

V-26) Liberation theology arose from the reflections of a Catholic priest in Peru—Fr. Gustavo Gutierrez—struggling with how he could comfort his parishioners who were oppressed by the predatory government common to Latin America during most of its history. His essential concept was the encouragement to parishioners that they form small church groups to support each other, develop their own solutions, become their own leaders, and work for change. This concept was adopted and expanded by Marxist oriented Catholics—laity and priests, many of whom became involved in the various revolutionary movements in the region—to mean that the central work of the Church is the poor, leading to a major crisis of the Church in the last century which Pope Benedict as Cardinal Ratzinger spent much time on when Prefect of the Congregation for the Doctrine of the Faith.

V-27) Liberation theology has been used by many in the Church to address criminal behavior for several decades. However, in its Marxist orientation it has caused more harm than good, as it has focused attention on structural social deficiencies rather than individual responsibility—external causation rather than internal choice and defining the criminal as the oppressed—leading many people down dead-end streets seeking solutions while the problem deepens.

V-28) Going beyond liberation theology is the development of criminal world leadership who will speak for, and create solutions for, themselves, freed from the self-contradictory Marxist core of liberation theology.

Going beyond liberation theology is realizing that there is no oppressor the criminal seeks relief from, for he is the oppressor.

Going beyond liberation theology is realizing that the only true liberation is from the greatest lie ever imagined to the greatest story ever told and while the great lie appears graspable and silkily real to touch, the great story only begins in a yearning hardly comprehended until the plot is unraveled, marked, and reformulated to fill the criminal's yearning soul.

V-29) The criminal seeking God—having already embraced the world and found promise in it—can only comprehend a God verifiable objectively, a God found in the prince of the world, seemingly concrete, solid and real as the sensuality of hedonism.

This path of liberation can only be *discovered* by the completely imprisoned criminal, for no criminal not so enmeshed can appreciate acceptance of eternity through the working of each day; but it can be only fully *practiced* by the completely free criminal, for no criminal having discovered true liberation can forever run from it.

V-30) Liberation theology began as a reflection on "faith without works is dead." Our Catholic faith, our baptism, our communion, is a reaffirmation that we are part of the People of God, working to bring others into the Kingdom of God, in the knowledge that Catholics with well-formed consciences will work for a better world and a singular aspect of a better world involves bringing our faith into the public square, voting it, expressing it, even to the point of personal danger, which in the cause of Christ—we are called to accept.

Going beyond liberation theology in the transformation of criminals is grasping the understanding that true doing can only follow true being.

Going beyond liberation theology is grasping the understanding that only one true theology exists and it is the theology of the real, the theology of the Catholic Church, ancient, wise, and eternal.

The eternal foundation upon which the Church rests is the sacredness of each real human life; not in the abstract, but in the specific sense of a real individual human being.

This foundation of the Church finds fulfillment in the summit of the Church during the daily Mass; where Christ enters again into each faithful human being during the real Eucharistic celebration.

This foundation also animates the international posture of the Church in the political arena through its eternal and very real responsibility to protect the innocent; whether through the call for the protection of the unborn, or through the violent exercise of a just war, or the legally proscribed use of capital punishment; and where the real politic stance of the abortionists or the pacifistic stance of the war and capital punishment abolitionists is an assault upon the foundation and the summit.

Within the founding spirit of the United States, the overwhelming focus is on the protection of human dignity, human freedom, and religious freedom; powerful marks for a great power to assume and very congruent with those of the other great power in the world—and the only real power capable of truly defeating the prince of this world—the Church Christ founded upon the rock of Peter.

V-31) A stranger is helped best by a friend. The deep knowledge leader is from the community of the stranger, but has become transformed. He knows the secrets of the stranger and now transformed, stands ready to help as a friend. When he becomes educated and credentialed, the formation of competence, he helps as a professional friend.

The solution is within the problem.

Subsidiarity asks that problems are best dealt with closest to their source. While social currents may affect the environment of social problems, it is the purely personal where we see most clearly their effect.

Helping the stranger means helping their struggle against their inclination to harm themselves, and this brings us into work of great peril, moment, and consequence, where the best guide is often someone having already trod the path.

Working within suffering redeemed is where spiritual power grows, and those who are called to work selflessly to help others, often at dizzying hourly days, are resolute. They get tired, sometimes to their very bones, but they are working within a power which is inexhaustible.

The great transformational saints of the streets, all of those known and unknown, realize that what keeps them strong in the face of the great suffering they see daily is the Christ they see in every human face.

Each day of their work is filled with the pain of others, each day of fatigue and silent weeping at the struggle to remain whole, each day on the cross grows the strength and endurance that is the stuff saints are made of.

V-32) Transformation is personal, based on love and surrender. For grassroots leaders it is the love of the other; surrendering to that love, and in their passion for seeing joy overwhelm suffering, they are transformed by the work.

The founding stone of the social teaching is the right to life for all human beings and all that entails; the right to the means to maintain life, to secure work and sustenance according to individual means, to educate ourselves to our potential, to associate with whom we wish, coming together to advocate for social change, and the right to dignity and justice.

We know this exists but rarely upon earth, yet knowing it is inalienably due each of us as creatures of God, and can irrevocably ground our work and give it strength of truth none can question.

But we are called to learn the root of these rights, and this is a duty which inalienable rights demand we shoulder; to learn, to study, and to grasp the shaded meanings and clarity of purpose upon which our work with others stands.

VI- Part Four
The Interior Journey

It is a long and often dark way, but the promise of light and freedom sparkling bright beyond me, eternally present, pulls me forward.

Deep Knowledge

Deep knowledge is the congruence of experiential knowledge, academic and professional learning; grounded and informed by extended study in the social teaching of the Catholic Church and participating in her sacramental life.

VI-1) Deep knowledge is the knowledge arising from the informed thought that comes from *being—being* preceding knowing.

Being a child of God, being a child of the Church—breathing with the Church—within the apostolate God established for you before time began, and learning all that can be learned from the world about the work of your apostolate; so that it infuses your *being,* that is deep knowledge.

VI-2) Why is the one who is lost and the prodigal son, so valuable to Christ?

Why is lost important?

Is it the supreme value placed on each person, or is it what the recovery of the lost returns to the whole, perhaps both?

The professional criminal, the battle-hardened soldier, the veteran street cop; each share an intimate knowledge of evil that even intellectual pyrotechnics cannot dislodge, and if they are Catholic and if they are coupling this experiential knowledge with that from the academy, professional training, a continual study of Catholic social teaching, and, applied to work for the common good connected to their life—this is deep knowledge and they can draw from this well, replenished with prayer, liturgy and contemplation, to bring many souls from Satan's grasp to Christ's Church.

VI-3) The deepest knowledge of all is the practice of the Church—where the saints aborning walk—within the church, daily communion, daily rosary, daily examination and prayers unceasing.

Daily Practice

Our soul, like a tuning fork, becomes congruent with God through daily practice and a daily life informed by that practice. Christ comes daily let us go to meet him.

VI-4) The transformation of criminals is work of great spiritual peril, and the transformed criminal aspiring to a community leadership role has to accept certain minimal experiential requirements that will counteract the reality of his criminal world experience with that of communal world experience; by having lived ten years out of prison and already helping the community; having obtained a graduate college degree; and being married to another Catholic.

He also has to daily reach for the deepest knowledge of all, which is the knowledge gained from continuous communion with God; the continual prayer and daily practice set forth by the reach for perfection to which each are called through our baptism and communion within the Kingdom of God.

VI-5) In olden times, the paths humans made to travel here and there were made by human feet, traveling the same way through the forest and over the plain as the day and year before, and as the years deepened the path, it became a hardened way that remained for guidance through the woods and mountains to the way home.

As it is with our own path, made daily through the rituals established by the Church to feed her saints and priests the food divine—morning prayer, communion, midday angelus, praying the rosary, evening prayer, examination of conscience, sacrifices to the Church, to God, to Peter, fighting against sin and building virtue; and through this daily practice, the armor of God is slowly crafted as the penitential, transformed criminal aspiring to community leadership—for whom this is a vital journey of lifetime penance from the years of harm caused to others through his criminality—enters into the hardened path of the priestly soul and saintly temperament on the long journey home.

VI-6) I was baptized in 2004, so am still in the process of learning about this universal community stretching through eons of time and encompassing so much temporal and spiritual space.

For many months the glow from my baptism carried me happily along in the observance of the sacramental life of the Church so familiar to Cradle Catholics, attending Sunday Mass regularly, supporting the Church, blending many of the rituals around the liturgical seasons into our daily life; but then as the glow from the baptism wore somewhat off I encountered a period of spiritual dryness.

My spiritual dryness came largely from the increased reading and study of the Catholic life in the United States and around the world, and as I began to see the human failures and satanic work in the priestly abuse of children; seemingly connected to the deep trough of relativism the Church in America and Europe had been wallowing in for several decades as she struggled to combat the enemies from within and without.

I began exploring membership in lay Catholic organizations which I felt would recapture the glow of baptism, but what I found was that, what I thought I needed from other Catholic organizations was something I only needed to *do* myself; embrace the daily practice of communion, prayer, and devotion. The spiritual dryness

I thought was calling me deeper back into the Church through lay organizational involvement was instead just a simple call back to the Church.

Since June 9, 2008 I have taken each step of the daily path faithfully and have been blessed and surprised how satisfying it has become and how much peace I've received from it.

For penitential criminals, so long in the service of the prince of this world, daily enrichment is necessary so that the companionship with Christ becomes a daily walking with him and the Church he founded upon the rock of Peter two thousand years ago.

In my inherent pride of self—temptingly strengthened through faithful attendance at daily mass proving the supremacy of my will—I am also reminded, almost daily, by Old Testament prophets or New Testament apostles and Christ not to become "Blind guides, who strain out the gnat and swallow a camel". (Matthew 23:23-26)

I also found, in the daily homiletic teaching from the priests of my parish, refreshment and broadening of spiritual grace that was deeply enhancing my individual journey into Catholicism as well as the sacramental grace received through daily reception of the Holy Eucharist.

However, the most wonderful grace is that received from being in the company of saints—Mass with the saints—both those whose stories we acknowledge each day, and the many saints surrounding me in the parish pews whose stories I do not know but whose faith and devotion to Holy Mother Church is so evident through their daily practice.

VI-7) The petition—"give us this day our daily bread"—in the *Our Father* began to acquire a different meaning for me after many months of daily mass and praying the rosary daily with its recitation of the prayer before each decade; becoming more eucharistic than earthly, and I discovered others had come to the same conclusion and beyond, then I understood that it was both; the saying of grace before partaking of the divine food, and the plea for today's earthly sustenance.

References to Christ as living water and bread of life are central to Catholic theology and the insertion of the petition about daily bread in the *Our Father*, said at every Mass, is congruent, leading to an injunction to daily eucharistic celebration.

VI-8) Women, who have been so marginalized throughout human history, yet retain the clarity of spirit—as did Mary, the mother of our Lord and Mary Magdalene—to see the truth; and it is they who are first in the daily mass, they who do almost all of the readings, they who mostly distribute the body and blood of our Lord; they the saints aborning, who I am privileged to be among each morning.

VI-9) The thoughts of the lowly matter— but of course—for there are no least in the Kingdom of God—only children of God.

Greatest children and the least of children with only purity of thought congruent with action separating them.

It is not only the greatest who are able to solve problems—and as Henry VIII proclaimed as he tore the English Church asunder: *"I can become what I will"*; and as American Manifest Destiny grew from the Protestant definition of success filtered through Harvard, Catholics knew it is God's will behind becoming.

Lectio Divina

Solidarity—a great teaching to contemplate—in its fullest sense would stand with all, rich and poor, criminal and saint, black and white.

VI-10) **The** practice of *lectio divina* (divine reading) is an ancient one, arising from the monasteries of the Church, and is a powerful form of contemplation carried out in daily life.

Reading a particular section of scripture and then contemplating it, praying about it, and discussing it, was the monastic way; but the way in which I use it can involve any reading from Church leaders— particularly the Holy Father—or Catholic scholars and working from the baseline of the magisterium and the work of the apostolate, dwell deeply on the idea for as much time as seems fruitful, often several days or weeks.

VI-11) There are so many ways people choose to perceive the singular reality, that we quickly realize Babel is not only still central to the experience of life in the world; but remains Satan's most cherished tool and God's greatest gift—the freedom to choose how we see—how we hear—how we speak—and it is here in this quiet contemplation and decision making around this that the ancient practice of Lectio Divina plays such a major role.

Lectio Divina is a Catholic tool of spiritual contemplation that can bring one into such deep communion with God—if it is part of the daily practice of prayer and devotions incumbent upon those desiring priestly souls—that if enough criminals entered into its darkness leading to light; even those within the super-max cells; eventually great and powerful blessings would flow upon the earth from their contemplative prayer.

VI-12) Solidarity—a great teaching to contemplate—in its fullest sense would stand with all, rich and poor, criminal and saint, black and white.

And the preferential option for the poor would be the solidarity option embracing the rich, for solidarity stands *against* no one, but *for* all.

A root of solidarity is friendship among groups of strangers transcending strangeness, binding us all by the common ground of our existence as human beings and creatures of God.

Solidarity is friendship, friendship of the highest level, grounded in the ancient ritual of sacrifice of self to another. The highest gift brings the greatest reward and laying down our earthly life is to have eternal life.

Our friends have created a home for us. Through countless ages, human beings of good will, self sacrifices, and eternal vision, have laid down their lives, fortunes, and dreams on the floor of our existence. It is a floor of enduring stone, built with divine goodness and familial love.

Solidarity between human beings is best expressed by speaking truth to one another and the great tears in its fabric come through the conscious wounding of that truth.

I remember, as do you, those moments when the face of the *Other* became the face of a friend and in that moment solidarity breathes through us with its ancient, warm familial breath.

We have become so materialistic that we preclude spiritual authenticity to all immersed in it, yet should we not also be in solidarity to those whose path to salvation is as passing through the eye of a needle, those who have become enemized by so many, and in solidarity with them fulfill our greatest commandment

VI-13) Now, as we go forth with God, let us look always to the boundaries of our lives for the call of truth laying there; and breaking through boundaries seek and acquire that deeper knowledge that—in its elemental form—is a continuation of the work Christ began, so powerfully even during his last moments when he canonized the first saint of the Catholic Church, the penitential criminal Dismas.

"With Peter, to Christ, through Mary, for the Greater Glory of God"

About the Author

David H. Lukenbill is a former criminal—thief and robber—who has transformed his life through education; an Associate of Arts degree in Administration of Justice from Sacramento City College, a Bachelor of Science degree in Organizational Behavior from the University of San Francisco, and a Master of Public Administration degree from the University of San Francisco; several years developing, managing, and consulting with criminal transformative organizations, and a conversion to Catholicism.

He is married to his wife of 26 years and they have one child. They live by the American River in California with two cats, and all the wild critters they can feed.

Contact information at the Lampstand Foundation website
www.lampstandfoundation.org

The Lampstand Foundation

The Lampstand Foundation is a 501 c (3) nonprofit corporation founded by David H. Lukenbill in Sacramento, California in 2003 as a lay apostolate grounded in the social teaching of the Catholic Church, to provide leadership development tools for community organizations—managed by reformed criminals—working to reform criminals.

Mission

Transforming the repentant criminal, suffering from his distance from God, into a deep knowledge leader who can teach other criminals the path to redemption through the social teaching of the Catholic Church.

God longs for the tears of criminals; He thirsts for the tears of sinners.

(St. John Chrysostom)

Prayer to St. Michael for Protection of The Catholic Church and Her Members

✠ Glorious St. Michael, Guardian and Defender of the Church of Jesus Christ, come to the assistance of the Church, against which the powers of Hell are unchained. Guard with thy special care her august visible head, and obtain for him and for us that the hour of triumph may speedily arrive.

✠ Glorious Archangel St. Michael, watch over us during life, defend us against the assaults of the demon, assist us especially at the hour of death, obtain for us a favorable judgment and the happiness of beholding God face to face for endless ages. Amen.

www.ingramcontent.com/pod-product-compliance
Lightning Source LLC
LaVergne TN
LVHW021540080426
835509LV00019B/2752